ALL ABOUT MY CAT.

ALSO BY PHILIPP KEEL

All About Me.

All About Me—Millennium Edition.

All About Us.

Look at Me

All About My Dog.

Technicolor

ALL ABOUT MY CAT.

BY PHILIPP KEEL

BROADWAY BOOKS

NEW YORK

BROADWAY

ALL ABOUT MY CAT. © 2003 by Philipp Keel. All rights reserved. No part of this book may be repro-
duced or transmitted in any form or by any means, electronic or mechanical, including photocopying,
recording, or by any information storage and retrieval system, without written permission from the pub-
lisher. For information, address Broadway Books, a division of Random House, Inc.

PRINTED IN THE UNITED STATES OF AMERICA

BROADWAY BOOKS and its logo, a letter B bisected on the diagonal, are trademarks of Random House,
Inc.

Visit our website at www.broadwaybooks.com

First edition published 2003.

Based on an original design by Philipp Keel

Library of Congress Cataloging-in-Publication Data has been applied for.

Thanks to Liz Keel

ISBN 0-7679-1494-5

10 9 8 7 6 5 4 3 2 1

Cats have an air of mystery that has captivated people for thousands of years. They were deities in ancient Egypt and symbols of the occult in Medieval Europe. And Chinese and Japanese mystics once believed that good people were reincarnated not as people, but as cats. With their self-confidence, quiet wisdom, and sly agendas, cats today may not be considered holy, but they are certainly independent and aristocratic, inspiring in us a deep-seated admiration and affection. No matter how aloof our cats may seem, they understand and entertain us with a wit and intelligence that seems almost human.

Your relationship with your cat is a constant reminder not only of the powerful bond between animals and humans but of how important it is to find a true meeting of the minds in all of our relationships. As you answer the questions in this book, you will be creating a thoughtful record of your cat's life and your years together that will not only reveal who you are as individuals but who you are together. It is my hope that the unique facts, opinions, and memories recorded will illuminate all the most special details that have made your lives together so unexpectedly interesting and delightful.

—Philipp Keel

CONTENTS

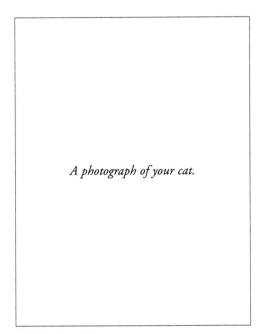

A photograph of your cat.

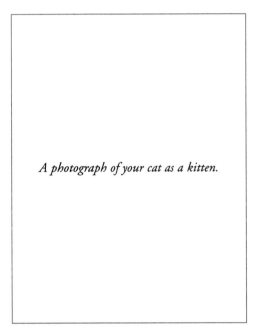

A photograph of your cat as a kitten.

ALL ABOUT MY CAT.

M Y C A T

Why do you have a cat? _____

_____

Your cat's name: _____

Date of birth (actual or estimated): _____

Place of birth: _____

Your cat is   ( ) female.   ( ) male.

Weight: _____

Fur color: _____

Eye color: _____

Distinct markings: _____

Occupation: _____

Extracurricular activities: _____

_____

Awards: _____

_____

M Y   C A T

Why did you pick your cat's name? _____

_____

Your favorite nickname for your cat: _____

If you had to choose a new name for your cat, what name would you pick from the following list?

    ( ) Pink   ( ) Ming   ( ) Una   ( ) Psycho   ( ) Circus
    ( ) Osky   ( ) Muffin   ( ) Snow   ( ) Charm   ( ) Lindbergh
    ( ) Spook   ( ) Hefner   ( ) Monday   ( ) Troja   ( ) Sony
    ( ) Fancy   ( ) Pepper   ( ) Lilly   ( ) Pout   ( ) Morning

( ) You found your cat.   ( ) Your cat found you.

You got your cat

    ( ) as a kitten in a pet store.   ( ) as a stray kitten from an animal shelter.
    ( ) as a kitten from a breeder.   ( ) as a kitten from a newspaper ad.
    ( ) as an adult in a pet store.   ( ) as a stray adult from an animal shelter.
    ( ) as an adult from a newspaper ad.   ( ) as an adult from a neighbor or friend.
    ( ) as a kitten from a neighbor or friend.

Three criteria for choosing a cat as a pet:

1 _____

2 _____

3 _____

M Y   C A T

Three things about your cat that made you choose her/him:

1 _____

2 _____

3 _____

Is your cat a pure breed?   ( ) Yes   ( ) No

If yes, what is the name of the breed? _____

Do you care about pedigree?   ( ) Yes   ( ) No

Did you always want that breed of cat?   ( ) Yes   ( ) No

If no, what kind of cat did you wish for? _____

If you couldn't have a cat, what animal (even if owning it as a pet is not realistic) would you like

to have? _____

What is your cat's parentage? _____

Describe your cat's appearance: _____

_____

Are you proud of your cat's appearance?   ( ) Yes   ( ) No

Do you look like your cat?   ( ) Yes   ( ) No

Your cat is

      ( ) a queen.   ( ) a spy.   ( ) a puff ball.
      ( ) a control freak.   ( ) a magician.   ( ) a Barbie.

Your cat is

      ( ) a city cat.   ( ) a suburban cat.   ( ) a country cat.

Your cat is

      ( ) an indoor cat.   ( ) an outdoor cat.
      ( ) an indoor and outdoor cat.

Another animal your cat sometimes resembles: _____

( ) You trained your cat.   ( ) Your cat trained you.

Your cat's astrological sign: _____

Do you think the sign matches her/his personality?   ( ) Yes   ( ) No

Your cat's motto: _____

_____

One word to describe your cat: _____

Your cat's biggest talent: _____

Your cat's character is most like which of the following?

( ) Cary Grant   ( ) Hello Kitty   ( ) Sean Penn   ( ) Gwyneth Paltrow
( ) Mahatma Gandhi   ( ) Marilyn Monroe   ( ) Bill Gates   ( ) Diane Keaton
( ) Steve Martin   ( ) Lance Armstrong   ( ) Lady Di   ( ) Sigmund Freud
( ) James Lipton   ( ) Aretha Franklin   ( ) Jack Nicholson   ( ) Jimmy Carter
( ) Sophia Loren   ( ) Sean Connery   ( ) Leonardo DiCaprio   ( ) Roy Orbison
( ) Julianne Moore   ( ) Oliver Hardy   ( ) Elizabeth Taylor   ( ) Joe Pesci
( ) Stevie Wonder   ( ) Greta Garbo   ( ) Richard Gere   ( ) Cher
( ) Hillary Rodham Clinton   ( ) Steven Spielberg   ( ) Madonna

Your cat would most like to have which of the following occupations?

( ) President   ( ) Playgirl/Playboy   ( ) Lawyer   ( ) Burglar   ( ) Actor
( ) Farmer   ( ) Personal Trainer   ( ) Psychoanalyst   ( ) Priest   ( ) Artist
( ) Teacher   ( ) Hair Stylist   ( ) Real Estate Broker   ( ) Social Worker
( ) Journalist   ( ) Food Critic   ( ) Pilot   ( ) Fisherman   ( ) CEO
Other: _____

What type of television entertainment does your cat prefer?

( ) Cartoons   ( ) Silent movies   ( ) Sitcoms   ( ) Westerns   ( ) Soap operas
( ) Action   ( ) Comedy   ( ) Drama   ( ) The Weather Channel   ( ) Musicals
( ) Documentaries   ( ) Talk shows   ( ) Reality TV   ( ) Game shows   ( ) News
( ) Cooking shows   ( ) Commercials

Which of the following musicians does your cat enjoy listening to the least?

( ) James Taylor   ( ) Snoop Dogg   ( ) Irving Berlin   ( ) Enya
( ) Sting   ( ) The Kelly Family   ( ) Eminem   ( ) Johannes Brahms
( ) Carlos Santana   ( ) Michael Jackson   ( ) Shania Twain
( ) Marilyn Manson   ( ) Barbra Streisand   ( ) Kenny G.   ( ) Tom Jones
( ) Ricky Martin   ( ) Ella Fitzgerald   ( ) Paul McCartney
( ) The Velvet Underground   ( ) Earth, Wind & Fire

Other: _____

Your cat's instincts are

( ) long gone.   ( ) dormant.   ( ) to wait until waited on.
( ) acute and helpful when hunting mice.
( ) sharp and impressive at all times.

Your cat is more like   ( ) a Republican.   ( ) a Democrat.

When your cat is lonely, she/he _____

When your cat is happy, she/he _____

When your cat is frightened, she/he _____

When your cat is feeling playful, she/he _____

Your cat is too proud to beg.   ( ) True   ( ) False

Your cat is really moody.   ( ) True   ( ) False

Your cat is nicer than you.   ( ) True   ( ) False

Your cat likes surprises.   ( ) True   ( ) False

Your cat is arrogant.   ( ) True   ( ) False

Your cat is independent.   ( ) True   ( ) False

Your cat needs you.   ( ) True   ( ) False

Your cat opens doors by her-/himself.   ( ) True   ( ) False

Your cat hates getting wet.   ( ) True   ( ) False

Your cat is appreciative.   ( ) True   ( ) False

Your cat is ambitious.   ( ) True   ( ) False

Your cat is modest.   ( ) True   ( ) False

Your cat is a poser.   ( ) True   ( ) False

Your cat easily gets offended.   ( ) True   ( ) False

Three of your cat's funniest habits:

1 _____

2 _____

3 _____

One thing that makes your cat crazy: _____

Something strangely human about your cat: _____

Early Morning: _____

8: _____

9: _____

10: _____

11: _____

Noon: _____

1: _____

2: _____

3: _____

4: _____

5: _____

6: _____

7: _____

8: _____

9: _____

10: _____

Late Night: _____

What is elegant about your cat? _____

What is your cat's best feature? _____

What is your cat's worst feature? _____

Your cat is   ( ) long haired.   ( ) short haired.

( ) Long-haired cats have more fun.   ( ) Short-haired cats have more fun.

Do you mind having your cat's fur on your clothing?   ( ) Yes   ( ) No

How much time per day does your cat spend grooming its fur?

    ( ) 10 minutes   ( ) 30 minutes   ( ) 1 hour   ( ) 5 hours

How often do you brush or comb your cat?

    ( ) Once a day   ( ) Once a week   ( ) Once a month
    ( ) Once a year   ( ) Never   ( ) Your cat likes a messy look

Do you take your cat to a groomer?   ( ) Yes   ( ) No

If yes, how often?

Your cat

    ( ) is quite concerned about her/his hygiene.
    ( ) is pretty careless about her/his cleanliness.
    ( ) pays a lot of attention to her/his beauty.
    ( ) doesn't really care about her/his looks.

Do you occasionally give your cat a manicure and pedicure? ( ) Yes ( ) No

If yes, ( ) your cat likes it. ( ) you like it.

What kind of collar does your cat like to wear? _____

Do you ever feel that your cat costs too much money? ( ) Yes ( ) No

How much would you estimate you spend on your cat's care every year? _____

A part of your cat's care that you don't like to pay for: _____

One thing you love to buy for your cat: _____

Does your cat enjoy luxury? ( ) Yes ( ) No

If yes, what kind of luxury? _____

What is the most expensive gift you ever gave your cat? _____

Name one thing you wish your cat could do on her/his own: _____

Name one thing you wish your cat could do for you: _____

How does your cat manipulate you? _____

How do you manipulate your cat? _____

Is your cat spoiled?   ( ) Yes   ( ) No

Three ways you spoil your cat:

1 _____

2 _____

3 _____

Not even the Egyptians would have worshipped your cat more than you do.   ( ) Definitely

How many toys does your cat have?

    ( ) Too many   ( ) Just enough   ( ) Less than other cats

List a few of your cat's toys: _____

_____

Your cat's most prized possession: _____

Have you ever played dress-up with your cat?   ( ) Yes   ( ) No

If yes, did your cat think it was fun?   ( ) Yes   ( ) No

Does your cat ever wear clothing?   ( ) Yes   ( ) No

If yes, list the items in your cat's wardrobe: _____

_____

Do you ever dance with your cat, holding her/his paws?   ( ) Yes   ( ) No

Does your cat have a cat condo?   ( ) Yes   ( ) No

A compliment you often give your cat: _____

_____

You prefer photographs of your cat

    ( ) in action.   ( ) posed.   ( ) in costumes.
    ( ) with family members.   ( ) sleeping.

If you could, what would you like to do for your cat at least once in her/his life? _____

_____

Your cat hunts only when hungry.   ( ) True   ( ) False

How does your cat stalk her/his prey? _____

_____

Is your cat a successful hunter or an amateur? _____

Your cat's ideal dinner: _____

_____

A special treat you give your cat: _____

Do you give your cat catnip?   ( ) Yes   ( ) No

You sometimes cook for your cat.   ( ) Yes   ( ) No

Your cat's taste is   ( ) finicky.   ( ) indiscriminate.

One word to describe your cat's table manners: _____

How much do you spend per week on your cat's food? _____

What do you feed your cat? _____

_____

What is your cat's favorite kind of people food? _____

Something strange that your cat once ate: _____

Something your cat refuses to eat: _____

The most amazing dish you have ever served your cat: _____

Does your cat like fruit or vegetables?   ( ) Yes   ( ) No

Does your cat enjoy scavenging in the garbage?   ( ) Yes   ( ) No

Does your cat lick food off your fingers?   ( ) Yes   ( ) No

How often do you feed your cat by hand? _____

Do you let your cat eat off the table?   ( ) Yes   ( ) No

Have your ever seen your cat eating something that she/he caught?   ( ) Yes   ( ) No

If yes, what did she/he catch? _____

Your cat is   ( ) too sleepy.   ( ) too active.

As a master, you are   ( ) too lazy.   ( ) too catering.

Three reasons why you are jealous of your cat's life:

1 _____

2 _____

3 _____

Do you sometimes wish you could switch roles with your cat?   ( ) Yes   ( ) No

Who is more lazy?

   ( ) You   ( ) Your cat   ( ) Your significant other

Your cat is in a cuddling mood

   ( ) when she/he has just been fed.
   ( ) after coming home from playing outside.
   ( ) when you stroke her/his fur.
   ( ) whenever she/he feels like it.
   ( ) only when she/he is sleepy.

When your cat rolls over on her/his back, it means _____

_____

Your cat prefers to lounge in the following rooms.

( ) The kitchen   ( ) The living room   ( ) The dining room
( ) The office   ( ) The children's room   ( ) The basement
( ) The attic   ( ) Your bedroom

Your cat's favorite piece of furniture: _____

A place from which your cat likes to observe: _____

An unusual place where your cat likes to rest: _____

What do you feel when your cat falls asleep on your lap? _____

_____

Do you kiss your cat good night?   ( ) Yes   ( ) No

If yes, where do you kiss your cat good night? _____

Does your cat like to be covered?   ( ) Yes   ( ) No

If yes, with what do you cover her/him? _____

Where does your cat sleep? _____

Do you like your cat to sleep in bed with you?   ( ) Yes   ( ) No

One word to describe your cat's sleep: _____

Does your cat make sounds when she/he sleeps?   ( ) Yes   ( ) No

How does your cat get you out of bed in the morning? _____

_____

When sleeping, your cat resembles

      ( ) a baby after getting the bottle.
      ( ) a retired tourist in Florida.   ( ) a countess.
      ( ) an expensive fur muff.   ( ) an uncle in a sun chair.
      ( ) a snobby supermodel with a hangover.

When sleeping, your cat probably dreams about: _____

A photograph of your cat sleeping.

Where do you and your cat live? _____

A place your cat would prefer to live: _____

If you moved into a smaller space, your relationship with your cat would be

    ( ) worse.   ( ) better.   ( ) the same.

Your cat sometimes thinks living with you is quite uneventful.   ( ) Probably   ( ) No way

Your cat feels more comfortable when the house has just been cleaned.   ( ) True   ( ) False

Your cat enjoys being alone.   ( ) True   ( ) False

When you go away for a trip, your good-byes with your cat most resemble which of the following movies:

    ( ) *Sophie's Choice*   ( ) *Casablanca*   ( ) *Titanic*
    ( ) *National Lampoon*   ( ) *Some Like It Hot*
    ( ) *Dumb and Dumber*   ( ) *The Three Amigos*
    ( ) *War of the Roses*   ( ) *Kramer vs. Kramer*
    ( ) *Gone With the Wind*   ( ) *Bambi*   ( ) *Fargo*

When you go on a vacation, do you usually take you cat with you?   ( ) Yes   ( ) No

If not, who takes care of your cat while you are gone? _____

Whom would your cat prefer to be taken care of when you are away? _____

Your cat sitter is

    ( ) a paid professional.
    ( ) better at caring for your cat than you are.
    ( ) someone you can trust to take great care of your cat.
    ( ) someone who may or may not be regular with feedings.
    ( ) the only one who will watch your cat for free.

When you are on vacation, how often do you think of your cat?

    ( ) Constantly   ( ) Once a day   ( ) Once or twice during the trip
    ( ) Unfortunately, hardly ever

Do you feel guilty when you leave your cat home alone?   ( ) Yes   ( ) No

Does your cat act distant when you come back after a long trip?   ( ) Yes   ( ) No

Three things you suspect your cat does when you are away:

1 _____

2 _____

3 _____

Does your cat play with her/his toys alone?   ( ) Yes   ( ) No

Three things about your cat that makes it hard to leave her/him behind:

1 _____

2 _____

3 _____

Three things about your cat that makes it easy to leave her/him behind:

1 _____

2 _____

3 _____

Something you suspect your cat does while you are away: _____

One bad thing you have caught your cat doing when you got back home: _____

_____

If you left the refrigerator open, what would you come home to find your cat had eaten? _____

_____

How do you greet your cat when you come home? _____

There are good cats and bad cats. _____( ) True   ( ) False

What does your cat hide in your closet or under your bed? _____

Describe a moment when your cat embarrassed you: _____

_____

Describe a moment when you were embarrassed by how you treated your cat: _____

_____

Something forbidden your cat has done: _____

Your cat wouldn't dare: _____

Someone who doesn't like your cat at all: _____

Why doesn't that person like your cat? _____

_____

What is the most frightening prey your cat ever brought home? _____

The most precious thing your cat has damaged: _____

The most expensive thing your cat has damaged: _____

C A T A S T R O P H E

Have you ever spanked your cat?   ( ) Yes   ( ) No

If yes, why? _____

You could not live with a cat who: _____

_____

How do you punish your cat if she/he behaves badly? _____

_____

How does your cat punish you if you behave badly? _____

_____

If for whatever reason you had to give away your cat, who would be the first person you would

want her/him to be adopted by: _____

Who would be the last person you would want your cat to be adopted by: _____

_____

Your cat reacts to commands in which of the following languages?

( ) English   ( ) Spanish   ( ) Hebrew   ( ) Chinese
( ) Japanese   ( ) Russian   ( ) Italian   ( ) French
( ) Portuguese   ( ) Arabic   ( ) Swedish   ( ) German
Other: _____

Which command do you say most to your cat? _____

What is the nicest thing you have ever said to your cat? _____

What is the worst thing you have ever said to your cat? _____

What is the nicest thing your cat has ever said to you? _____

What is the rudest thing your cat has ever said to you? _____

Do you curse at your cat?   ( ) Yes   ( ) No

If yes, do you remember the worst curse you have ever used? _____

How does your cat fight with you? _____

What do you and your cat disagree on? _____

_____

Does your cat sometimes mix up the words "yes" and "no"?   ( ) Yes   ( ) No

If yes, do you think she/he secretly knows the difference?   ( ) Yes   ( ) No

When your cat won't listen, your show of authority most resembles which of the following figures?

( ) Napoleon   ( ) Your mother   ( ) Your father
( ) Nelson Mandela   ( ) Mr. Rogers   ( ) Beaver Cleaver
( ) Joan Crawford   ( ) Joseph Stalin   ( ) Martina Navratilova
( ) The Dalai Lama   ( ) The Germans   ( ) Genghis Khan
( ) Margaret Thatcher   ( ) Mother Teresa   ( ) Fidel Castro
( ) Carol Brady   ( ) Siegfried or Roy   ( ) Hulk Hogan

Have you ever wished your cat could talk?   ( ) Yes   ( ) No

If your cat could talk, what would she/he say to you? _____

_____

What do you feel when your cat says "meow"? _____

_____

Your cat's squeak means: _____

Your cat's howl means: _____

Your cat's growl means: _____

Your cat's purr means: _____

Your cat's snarl means: _____

Your cat's shriek means: _____

MEOWOLOGY

Your cat's silent meow means: _____

Your cat's chirp means: _____

When your cat is angry, she/he _____

_____

When your cat wants attention, she/he _____

_____

When your cat wants to be fed, she/he _____

_____

Why does your cat swish her/his tail? _____

_____

One word to describe your cat's voice: _____

One word to describe your cat's body language: _____

What makes your cat purr? _____

_____

Your cat greets you

( ) with its tail.　( ) with a kiss.　( ) with a "meow."
( ) with a rub.　( ) with a scratch.　( ) with a jump.

Does your cat often cry?　( ) Yes　( ) No

If yes, what is she/he crying about? _____

_____

Does your cat often laugh?　( ) Yes　( ) No

If yes, what is she/he laughing about? _____

_____

Do you hiss or bark at your cat?　( ) Yes　( ) No

Three things you had to teach your cat:

1 _____

2 _____

3 _____

Three things your cat knew without being taught:

1 _____

2 _____

3 _____

Three things your cat had to teach you:

1 _____

2 _____

3 _____

If your cat went to college, she/he would most likely study

( ) philosophy.   ( ) marine biology.   ( ) astronomy.
( ) art history.   ( ) fashion design.   ( ) literature.
( ) religion.   ( ) theater.   ( ) engineering.   ( ) economics.
( ) psychology.   ( ) music.   ( ) architecture.

Your cat would be   ( ) the teacher's pet.   ( ) the class clown.

Your cat would most likely prefer which of the following writers?

( ) Ayn Rand   ( ) T. S. Eliot   ( ) Freidrich Nietzsche
( ) Henry Miller   ( ) Jack Kerouac   ( ) Virginia Woolf
( ) William Faulkner   ( ) Sylvia Plath   ( ) J. D. Salinger
( ) Truman Capote

When your cat howls, it sounds like she/he is singing

( ) opera.   ( ) rap.   ( ) love songs.   ( ) reggae.
( ) rock 'n' roll.   ( ) country ballads.   ( ) gospel.
( ) bluegrass.   ( ) jazz or blues.

If your cat was on *Jeopardy*, what would her/his best category be? _____

If your cat was a writer,

she/he would write   ( ) fiction.   ( ) nonfiction.   ( ) poetry.

she/he would be   ( ) successful.   ( ) not very successful.

she/he would be a heavy drinker.   ( ) Yes   ( ) No

she/he would smoke   ( ) a pipe.   ( ) cigarettes.   ( ) a joint.

she/he would need   ( ) a muse.   ( ) a mouse.

If your cat could paint, her/his work would be   ( ) figurative.   ( ) abstract.

If your cat chose a career in show business, she/he would most likely

      ( ) appear in cat food commercials.
      ( ) write a musical called *Cats*.
      ( ) star in a family film.
      ( ) host a pet show.
      ( ) voice-over a character in a Disney animation.
      ( ) produce a show called *How to Be a Cat*.

How does your cat imitate you? _____

_____

How would you impersonate your cat? _____

_____

Your cat can

      ( ) turn door handles.   ( ) climb a ladder.
      ( ) open cupboards.   ( ) entertain your friends.
      ( ) ski.   ( ) make a phone call.   ( ) turn off the stereo.
      ( ) understand your parents.   ( ) inflate a balloon.
      ( ) read *The New Yorker*.

Does your cat demonstrate any of the following paranormal abilities?

( ) Hypnosis ( ) Seduction ( ) Psychoanalysis
( ) Telepathy ( ) Winning the lottery ( ) Telekinesis
( ) Detecting spirits ( ) Brainwashing ( ) Levitation
( ) Leading a country ( ) Glowing in the dark

Where does your cat like to hide? _____

How does your cat tease you? _____

C A T ' S   R I G H T S

What do you do if your cat is sitting where you want to sit? _____

Who should not have a cat? _____

Every cat is born with the following three rights:

1 _____

2 _____

3 _____

Is your cat lucky to have you as an owner?   ( ) Yes   ( ) No

If yes, why? _____

How big is your cat's territory? _____

When does your cat fight? _____

Did your cat have the right to decide if she/he wanted to be
an indoor cat or an outdoor cat?   ( ) Yes   ( ) No

The idea of your cat on a leash is _____

The idea of your cat with no claws is _____

Does your cat have the right not to be spayed or neutered?   ( ) Yes   ( ) No

Something you would hate to see happen to your cat: _____

_____

Your cat should fight, if: _____

_____

How much money would it take for you to sell your cat?

    ( ) You would never sell your cat.   ( ) $50   ( ) $5,000
    ( ) $25,000   ( ) $100,000   ( ) $250,000   ( ) $1,000,000
    ( ) You would give her/him away for free, but no one is interested.

One moment when you wanted to get rid of your cat: _____

_____

Is your cat happy at the moment?   ( ) Yes   ( ) No

If no, why not? _____

_____

Most of the time, your cat is   ( ) pessimistic.   ( ) optimistic.

How does she/he demonstrate this quality? _____

_____

Your cat is

    ( ) wild.   ( ) domesticated.   ( ) civilized.

What does your cat think of the world? _____

_____

What is your cat's biggest inner conflict? _____

_____

You care more   ( ) about your cat.   ( ) about people (family not included).

Does your cat suffer from separation anxiety?   ( ) Yes   ( ) No

If yes, how does it show? _____

_____

Does your cat get scared easily?   ( ) Yes   ( ) No

What scares your cat the most? _____

_____

Does your cat sense when you are taking her/him to the veterinarian?   ( ) Yes   ( ) No

If yes, how does your cat react? _____

_____

You can think like a cat.   ( ) Yes   ( ) No

Do you believe that your cat realizes when you insult her/him?   ( ) Yes   ( ) No

It hurts your cat's feelings when you (check all that apply)

    ( ) push her/him off the sofa.   ( ) won't let her/him follow you into the bathroom.
    ( ) ignore her/his cries at the door.   ( ) won't give her/him a second helping of food.
    ( ) put her/him on a diet.

( ) You analyze your cat more.   ( ) Your cat analyzes you more.

Do you talk to your cat about your problems? ( ) Yes ( ) No

If yes, how does your cat help you? _____

_____

Is your cat a substitute for something you are missing? ( ) Yes ( ) No

If yes, try to describe what you are missing in one word: _____

What is neurotic about your cat? _____

What are your cat's pet peeves? _____

_____

What is your cat's little addiction? _____

You cat's biggest complaint about humans: _____

_____

A dramatic change in your cat's behavior was caused by: _____

_____

A dramatic change in your cat's weight was caused by: _____

_____

The source of your cat's anxiety could be

      ( ) traumatic kittenhood experiences.
      ( ) your neurotic behavior.   ( ) poor training.
      ( ) her/his breed disposition.   ( ) rude children.
      ( ) lack of attention.   ( ) fear of traffic.
      ( ) that she/he was a stray cat.   ( ) fear of dogs.
      ( ) waiting too long between meals.   ( ) change of season.

Your cat's biggest secret: _____

_____

Describe your cat in a traveling case: _____

_____

Have you ever drugged your cat before traveling with her/him?   ( ) Yes   ( ) No

Traveling with your cat for long distances is

     ( ) fun.   ( ) dangerous to your cat's health.   ( ) natural.
     ( ) stupid.   ( ) a hassle.   ( ) cruel.   ( ) adventurous.

Were you ever afraid a trip with your cat might threaten her/his life?   ( ) Yes   ( ) No

Has your cat ever been on an airplane?   ( ) Yes   ( ) No

If yes, how many times? _____

If yes, your cat was   ( ) in the cabin.   ( ) in the cargo compartment.

If your cat traveled in the cabin, was she/he scared during takeoff?   ( ) Yes   ( ) No

If your cat was stowed in the cargo compartment, how did you feel about that during the flight?

_____

_____

Was your cat angry with you when you met her/him at the baggage claim?   ( ) Yes   ( ) No

Has your cat ever been on a train?   ( ) Yes   ( ) No

Would your cat enjoy riding in a convertible?   ( ) Yes   ( ) No

If you drive with your cat, where does she/he sit? _____

_____

How many states has your cat seen? _____

What was your cat's favorite state? _____

List the countries your cat has visited: _____

_____

What is your cat's favorite country? _____

Does you cat seem to like different cultures?   ( ) Yes   ( ) No

A culture you think your cat would love to be a part of: _____

If your cat has never left home, why don't you travel with your cat? _____

_____

Have you ever lost your cat during a vacation? _____

Your cat's reaction to snow: _____

Your cat's reaction to rain: _____

Does your cat enjoy a barbeque at a rest area?   ( ) Yes   ( ) No

Your cat's behavior when you stop at a scenic point: _____

_____

Your cat appreciates visiting

    ( ) national monuments.   ( ) drive-throughs.
    ( ) museums.   ( ) national parks.   ( ) malls.
    ( ) antique fairs.   ( ) theme parks.   ( ) diners.

Your cat most appreciates driving

    ( ) over a mountain.   ( ) through a forest.   ( ) across a river.
    ( ) through a city.   ( ) along the sea.   ( ) through a desert.
    ( ) across the Great Plains.   ( ) through a tunnel.

When you stay in hotels with your cat, do you seek hotels that welcome animals or do you try to

sneak your cat in? _____

Have you ever been caught smuggling your cat to the room?   ( ) Yes   ( ) No

Your cat's ideal vacation: _____

_____

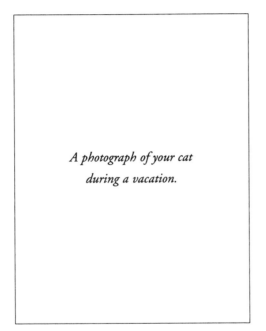

A photograph of your cat
during a vacation.

Your cat's hero: _____

Which is your cat's favorite holiday?

( ) Hanukkah   ( ) Christmas   ( ) Kwanza
( ) New Year's Day   ( ) Martin Luther King Day
( ) Valentine's Day   ( ) Holi   ( ) Easter   ( ) Passover
( ) Cinco de Mayo   ( ) Memorial Day   ( ) Birthdays
( ) Independence Day   ( ) Labor Day   ( ) Rosh Hashanah
( ) Ramadan   ( ) Halloween   ( ) Veterans' Day
( ) Thanksgiving
Other: _____

Where does your cat prefer to be petted? _____

_____

Are you your cat's favorite person?   ( ) Yes   ( ) No

Does your cat believe she/he is your favorite?   ( ) Yes   ( ) No

Your cat's favorite activity is

( ) hunting.   ( ) scratching fabrics.   ( ) running.
( ) stalking rodents.   ( ) schmoozing.   ( ) hiding.
( ) chasing strings and ribbons.   ( ) showing off.
( ) pouncing.   ( ) strolling.   ( ) climbing a tree.
( ) bunny-kicking toys.   ( ) annoying you.
( ) perching on a windowsill.
Other: _____

What does your cat enjoy most?

( ) Socializing with other cats   ( ) Socializing with other pets
( ) Socializing with humans   ( ) Being alone with toys
( ) Being alone in nature

What is your cat's favorite surface?

( ) Grass   ( ) Carpet   ( ) Marble   ( ) Linoleum   ( ) Gravel
( ) Hardwood floor   ( ) Fabric   ( ) Tree bark   ( ) Soil
( ) Asphalt   ( ) Ceramic tiles

Your cat's favorite thing to scratch: _____

Your cat's favorite TV show: _____

Your cat's favorite movie: _____

Your cat's favorite celebrity: _____

Your cat's favorite music or singer: _____

Your cat's favorite time of day: _____

Your cat's favorite waste of time: _____

Your cat's favorite place to think: _____

Your cat's favorite breakfast: _____

Your cat's favorite lunch: _____

Your cat's favorite dinner: _____

Your cat's favorite game: _____

Your cat's favorite indoor hobby: _____

Your cat's favorite outdoor hobby: _____

Your cat's favorite smell: _____

Your cat's favorite material or fabric: _____

Your cat's favorite object to contemplate: _____

Your cat's favorite thing to steal: _____

Your cat's favorite thing to bite: _____

Your cat's favorite thing to catch: _____

Your cat's favorite thing to torture: _____

Your cat's favorite artist would be: _____

Your cat's favorite cat: _____

The best day of your cat's life: _____

_____

How do you think your cat would describe you? _____

_____

Your cat is   ( ) more affectionate.   ( ) more independent.

Who is more loyal?

    ( ) You   ( ) Your cat   ( ) Your significant other

Do you think your cat misses her/his mother?   ( ) Yes   ( ) No

Your cat might think you are her/his mother.   ( ) Yes   ( ) No

What fascinates you most about the relationship between you and your cat? _____

_____

Mark three things you and your cat have in common:

    ( ) Codependent   ( ) Fussy   ( ) Dreamers   ( ) Realists
    ( ) Intuitive   ( ) Wise   ( ) Sophisticated   ( ) Lovable
    ( ) Antisocial   ( ) Particular   ( ) Warm-hearted
    ( ) Bothered by loud noises   ( ) Quirky   ( ) Boring
    ( ) Tidy   ( ) Socialites   ( ) Street smart   ( ) Modest
    ( ) Friendly   ( ) Scavengers   ( ) Arrogant   ( ) Stupid
    ( ) Well-mannered   ( ) Detached   ( ) Demanding
    ( ) Sweet   ( ) Noble   ( ) Cheap   ( ) Cool   ( ) Sincere

Do you sometimes envy your cat?   ( ) Yes   ( ) No

If yes, why? _____

_____

Does your cat sense what mood you are in?   ( ) Yes   ( ) No

Which day of the week does your cat cheer you up most?

    ( ) Sunday   ( ) Monday   ( ) Tuesday   ( ) Wednesday
    ( ) Thursday   ( ) Friday   ( ) Saturday

Does your cat understand what you want?   ( ) Yes   ( ) No

Do you understand what your cat wants?   ( ) Yes   ( ) No

Most of the time you feel like you and your cat are

    ( ) on the same team.   ( ) not on the same team.

What is the most unusual gift your cat ever brought to you? _____

When you are lonely, your cat _____

_____

When you are happy, your cat _____

_____

When you are frightened, your cat: _____

_____

When you are feeling playful, your cat: _____

_____

Do you feel that your cat is adopting your personality? ( ) Yes ( ) No

If yes, how does it show? _____

_____

Do you feel that you are adopting your cat's personality? ( ) Yes ( ) No

If yes, how does it show? _____

_____

Your cat ignores you when: _____

You ignore your cat when: _____

Your cat loves you when: _____

You love your cat when: _____

You spend

( ) enough time with your cat.
( ) not enough time with your cat.
( ) too much time with your cat.

How often do you play with your cat?

( ) Every day   ( ) At least once a week   ( ) Once a month
( ) When you feel like it   ( ) Unfortunately, not enough
( ) Hardly ever

Has your cat ever turned on you while playing?   ( ) Yes   ( ) No

Has your cat ever scratched you badly?   ( ) Yes   ( ) No

If yes, how did you react? _____

_____

Has your cat ever stolen anything from you?   ( ) Yes   ( ) No

If yes, what? _____

Where does sharing with your cat end? _____

Have you ever yelled at your cat and felt guilty afterward?   ( ) Yes   ( ) No

What prompted you to yell at your cat? _____

_____

One cat is enough. ( ) Yes ( ) No

At the end of your cat's life, you might say she/he was more a friend than a pet because of what

reason? _____

_____

A photograph of you and your cat.

Your cat is most social

      ( ) with you.   ( ) with children.   ( ) with other cats.
      ( ) with strangers.   ( ) with dogs.

When you have company, your cat tends to act

      ( ) discreet.   ( ) pushy.   ( ) insulted.
      ( ) welcoming.   ( ) arrogant.   ( ) humble.   ( ) territorial.
      ( ) casual.   ( ) polite.   ( ) rude.

Someone your cat enjoys hissing at: _____

How do you react when your cat hisses at guests? _____

How does it make you feel when your cat is overly affectionate with a guest? _____

_____

If a guest doesn't like your cat,

      ( ) you don't like your guest.
      ( ) you lock your cat in another room.
      ( ) you let your cat prowl around inconspicuously.
      ( ) you ask your guest if she/he is allergic.
      ( ) you try to demonstrate how special your cat is.

Has anyone ever had an allergic reaction to your cat?   ( ) Yes   ( ) No

If yes, who? _____

A member of your family or a friend with whom your cat loves to spend time: _____

_____

S O C I A L   C L I M B E R

A member of your family or a friend whom your cat completely ignores: _____

_____

Who are your cat's real friends? _____

Does your cat have a boyfriend or girlfriend?   ( ) Yes   ( ) No

If yes, who? _____

Has your cat ever had sex?   ( ) Yes   ( ) No

If yes, did it change her/his attitude? _____

Do you have other animals in the house besides your cat?   ( ) Yes   ( ) No

If yes, what is their relationship like? _____

_____

Which of the following pets does your cat generally dislike?

    ( ) Dog   ( ) Cat   ( ) Rabbit   ( ) Fish   ( ) Guinea pig
    ( ) Rat   ( ) Bird   ( ) Hamster   ( ) Mouse   ( ) Lizard
    ( ) Cow   ( ) Horse
    Other: _____

Does your cat have any enemies in your neighborhood (including people)?   ( ) Yes   ( ) No

Has your cat ever been attacked by another animal?   ( ) Yes   ( ) No

If yes, what happened? _____

_____

Try to describe the difference between "cat people" and "dog people" in one sentence: _____

_____

Cat people are: _____

Dog people are: _____

If your significant other hated your cat,

    ( ) you would end the relationship.
    ( ) you would get rid of your cat.

Do you mind your cat being in the same room when you are
intimate with someone?   ( ) Yes   ( ) No

If yes, why? _____

Do you mind your cat visiting you in the bathroom?   ( ) Yes   ( ) No

If yes, why? _____

Whom would you like your cat to be able to meet? _____

HEALTH & WELLNESS

Your veterinarian's name: _____

How did you choose your veterinarian? _____

_____

How do you know when your cat is sick? _____

How does your cat being sick affect your everyday life? _____

_____

If you make an extra effort, is your cat appreciative of your caretaking?   ( ) Yes   ( ) Not really

If yes, is your cat thankful?   ( ) Yes   ( ) No

Has your cat ever been really sick?   ( ) Yes   ( ) No

If yes, what kind of illness did she/he have? _____

Has your cat ever been on antibiotics?   ( ) Yes   ( ) No

Does your cat have serious health problems?   ( ) Yes   ( ) No

If yes, what is the problem with your cat's health? _____

Has your cat ever been injured?   ( ) Yes   ( ) No

If yes, how did she/he get injured? _____

Have you ever thanked God when your cat survived a disease,
an injury, or an accident?   ( ) Yes ( ) No

Did your cat ever have to wear a plastic collar around her/his neck?   ( ) Yes ( ) No

If yes, why? _____

Your cat has been spayed or neutered.   ( ) Yes ( ) No

Your cat has been declawed.   ( ) Yes ( ) No

Do you think your cat is a hypochondriac?   ( ) Yes ( ) No

What is your cat allergic to? _____

Has your veterinarian ever suggested a diet for your cat?   ( ) Yes ( ) No

If yes, how did it affect her/his mood, behavior and/or well-being? _____

_____

While on her/his diet, your cat

    ( ) was grumpier than an old man.
    ( ) was in shape like never before.
    ( ) turned into a nerve-wracking diva.
    ( ) was so offended that she/he gave you the silent treatment.
    ( ) escaped and went to Burger King.

How often does your cat expect you to clean her/his litter box?

    ( ) After each visit.   ( ) After a few visits.
    ( ) Your cat is very tolerant.   ( ) Your cat doesn't give a shit.

If you don't live up to your cat's litter box standards,

    ( ) she/he discreetly hides it under your furniture.
    ( ) she/he intentionally visits your closet.
    ( ) she/he pays a visit to the neighbor cat's litter box.
    ( ) she/he scrapes out the litter box as a temporary measure.

Do you sometime force your cat to take a bath?   ( ) Yes   ( ) No

Does your cat have bad breath?   ( ) Yes   ( ) No

If yes, is there anything you do to help it? _____

If someone invented a sauna for cats, would you buy one?   ( ) Yes   ( ) No

Do you sometimes massage your cat?   ( ) Yes   ( ) No

If yes, is your cat ticklish?   ( ) Yes   ( ) No

What do you do to keep your cat healthy? _____

_____

What do you do to keep your cat in shape? _____

_____

You would never have your cat put to sleep, unless: _____

_____

When your cat passes away, you will: _____

_____

B L A C K   C A T

A myth about cats you believe: _____

_____

When a black cat crosses your path, what do you think or do? _____

_____

Your cat is   ( ) lucky.   ( ) unlucky.

Does your cat always land on her/his feet?	( ) Yes ( ) No
Do you think your cat has ever fallen when you were not looking?	( ) Yes ( ) No
Do tabbies have more fun?	( ) True ( ) False
All calicoes are female.	( ) True ( ) False
Cats can see in the dark.	( ) True ( ) False
Stepping over a cat brings bad luck.	( ) True ( ) False
When a cat's whiskers droop, it's going to rain.	( ) True ( ) False
When a black cat jumps on the bed of a sick person, it means death is approaching.	( ) True ( ) False
Cats eat plants when they are sick.	( ) True ( ) False
Dreaming of a white cat means good luck.	( ) True ( ) False

A strange black cat on your porch brings prosperity. ( ) True ( ) False

When a black cat crosses the street, men "reposition" themselves. ( ) True ( ) False

A cat sleeping with all four paws tucked under means cold weather is coming. ( ) True ( ) False

When moving to a new home, always put the cat through the window instead of the door, so that she/he will not leave. ( ) True ( ) False

Witches and cats speak the same language. ( ) True ( ) False

An elderly cat frisking about means that a storm is brewing. ( ) True ( ) False

Cats have good balance because they are sensitive to Earth's magnetic field. ( ) True ( ) False

Cats predict hurricanes and earthquakes. ( ) True ( ) False

Do you believe that a cat has nine lives? ( ) Yes ( ) No

If yes, how many lives has your cat lived? _____

Describe your cat's most interesting past life: _____

_____

If you think your cat had a past life, do you feel that you might have known each other?   ( ) Yes   ( ) No

If yes, who was the master in your former relationship? ( ) You   ( ) Your cat

ALL ABOUT MY CAT

Do you think you will see your cat in an afterlife?   ( ) Yes   ( ) No

What is your cat's idea of hell? _____

_____

What is your cat's idea of heaven? _____

_____

One word to describe your cat's future: _____

What is going to be your cat's legacy? _____

_____

Tell someone who doesn't like cats one important thing she/he should know. _____

_____

Your most meaningful experience with your cat: _____

_____

What is the most important thing you have learned from your cat? _____

_____

Your most beautiful memory when your cat was a kitten: _____

_____

Your most special memory with your cat so far: _____

_____

What do you wish for your cat? _____

_____

What do you wish for your cat to wish for you? _____

_____

Your cat is better than the average cat.   ( ) Are you kidding?   ( ) You wish.

Cats are better than dogs.   ( ) True   ( ) False

Your cat is the best thing that ever happened to you.   ( ) Yes

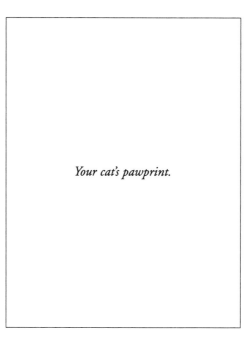

Your cat's pawprint.

Medical Record: _____

_____

_____

Feeding Notes: _____

_____

_____

Breeding Record: _____

_____

_____

Date of neutering: _____

Pregnancies: _____

_____

_____

Date of first birth: _____

Number of kittens in the litter: _____

Names, identifying colors, and markings of each kitten: _____

_____

_____

_____

_____

Date of second birth: _____

Number of kittens in the litter: _____

Names, identifying colors, and markings of each kitten: _____

_____

_____

_____

_____

ALL ABOUT MY CAT